Detective Dog went to Dave's Diner
every day for dinner.

For dessert, Detective Dog
always ordered a doughnut.
Detective Dog LOVED doughnuts.

One day after dinner, Detective Dog said to Dave,
"Today is my birthday. I think I will have
TWO doughnuts for dessert to celebrate."
"On the double, detective," said Dave.

"Oh, dear!" Dave cried.
"The doughnuts have disappeared!"
"Doggone it!" said Detective Dog.
"I have some detecting to do!"

Suddenly, Detective Dog noticed something
near the door. Powdered sugar!
"If I follow this trail of doughnut dust,
I bet I'll find the thief!" she said.

Detective Dog followed the trail
of doughnut dust downtown.

She followed it past Drake's Drugstore
and the department store.

The trail lead right into Debbie's Deli.
"The doughnut-napper must be in here!"
said Detective Dog.

Detective Dog turned the doorknob.
She stepped inside the deli.
It was completely dark.

Suddenly, the light flashed on.
"SURPRISE!" yelled Detective Dog's friends.

"Hot diggity dog!" said the detective.
"It's a birthday party!"

Dave told Detective Dog that he only
pretended the doughnuts had disappeared.
Dave made the trail of doughnut dust
to lead the detective to the party.

12

Detective Dog was delighted with the party.
There were dazzling decorations and dandy gifts.
And best of all, there were dozens and dozens
of delicious doughnuts!

How many things can you find that begin with the letter D?

See inside back cover for answers.

15

Dd Cheer

D is for dog and doughnut, too

D is for dolphin in the ocean blue

D is for doll, doctor, and door

D is for duck and dinosaur

Hooray for D, big and small—

the most dazzling, delightful letter of all!